SO YOU WANT TO RUN FOR POLITICAL OFFICE

A Practical Guide for Aspiring Politicians

by Robert "Dan" England, Jr.

Copyright, 1992 by Robert "Dan" England, Jr.
All Rights Reserved
First Edition: June 1992

Greenfield Center Press
3 Brookstone Drive
Greenfield Center, NY 12833
(518) 893-7974

Printed by Coneco Litho Graphics
Glens Falls, New York

ISBN 0-9633671-0-2

ACKNOWLEDGMENTS

I would like to thank my wife, Donna, and my father, Robert England, for their support and advice while I was writing this book.

I would also like to thank the following people who reviewed the first drafts of this book and offered suggestions for improvement:

—Laurel Quaid

—Esaw Peterson

—Michael Kearney

—Todd Popham

—Dr. George J. Gordon

—Joe Eshleman

CONTENTS

Introduction ... 5

PART I—PREPARATION

Chapter 1: Choosing an Office 11
Chapter 2: Shortcuts to Office 19
Chapter 3: Putting on Your Best Face 25
Chapter 4: Laying the Groundwork 33
Chapter 5: Choosing a Campaign Manager ... 41
Chapter 6: Getting Started 47
Chapter 7: Building The Campaign Organization 55
Chapter 8: Strategy 61

PART II—THE CAMPAIGN

Chapter 9: Early Campaign Activities 71
Chapter 10: Middle Campaign Activities 81
Chapter 11: Final Campaign Activities/ The Countdown 97
Chapter 12: Summary 107
Epilogue 113
Appendix 1 115

This book is dedicated to dreamers.

"...if one advances confidently in the direction of his dreams, and endeavors to live the life which he has imagined, he will meet with a success unexpected in common hours.

...If you have built castles in the air, your work need not be lost; that is where they should be. Now put the foundations under them."

Henry David Thoreau—*Walden*

INTRODUCTION

There are thousands of elected political offices in the USA today. If you would like to win one of these positions, you need a plan to get started. This book was written with you in mind. If you are an experienced political pro, you may want to pick and choose what you read. But if you are new to the political game, read on. In fact, I recommend you read this book several times and refer back to it often as your campaign progresses.

First, a little of my background. I became interested in politics in high school. I dreamed of running for office and making a difference in the world. I believed in John Kennedy and his call to "Ask not what your country can do for you; ask what you can do for your country." Today I'm still keenly interested in politics and read all I can about it.

I studied political science at Penn State. While on campus, I served on the student court as well as on my class advisory board. My first political lesson was learned while I worked on a campaign for student body president. But more of that later.

After receiving my undergraduate degree, I began working for the State Farm Insurance Companies as a supervisor in the Pennsylvania Regional office. (1969) My political interest lay dormant until I moved to the corporate headquarters in Bloomington Illinois. While there, I started night school working on a master's degree in Political Science at Illinois State University in Normal, Illinois, which I completed in 1983.

My first actual "real" campaign was working with a committee to elect a town council person in Normal Illinois. From that came an opportunity to run for Republican Precinct Committeeman against an incumbent. I won after knocking on almost every door in the precinct one chilly spring. That started a cycle of serious involvement in politics: campaign committees, political clubs, state conventions, Republican County Newsletter Editor and finally being appointed and re-elected twice to the McLean County Illinois Board until I was transferred by State Farm to their North Atlantic Office in Ballston Spa, New York, in 1991. As this book was written, I was scouting the political territory, using the principles of the book myself to get back into the game I love. In the first months in New York I helped design a winning campaign for a local school board race. Later, I worked on the campaign committee for a city council candidate.

Although my political life had been "part time," in many ways, politics for several years had become a full-time commitment.

Often times, after I received an angry call from a constituent late in the evening, I asked myself: "Is it worth it?"—especially since the pay is meager. I believe the answer is a resounding "yes"; for I have learned that, if you want to, you can make a difference—although I realize that many people would not agree with me. According to a Kettering Foundation Study, people "want to participate, but they believe there is no room for them in the political process they now know." (*Peoria Journal Star,* June 5, 1991, p1.) This book is intended to show you how you can be elected and make a place for yourself in the political process.

By being an elected official, you have the opportunity to influence and make policy in your community. For example, I helped in the passage of a new tax-supported fund to help mentally deficient persons in the county.

Holding office is gratifying and a great deal of the time it is fun. Just a note: If you want to run for office for the money, for glory or to enhance you career, you'd best think again. It hasn't happened that way for me or for most local politicians I know. Do it because you like it. Well, enough of my jabbering. Let's get to the business of getting you elected to office.

This book is organized in two parts. Part I—Preparation includes chapters 1–8. This will help you get ready for the political campaign. Part II—The Campaign includes chapters 9–11 and will help you plan activities that should take place during a campaign. The whole book is organized in chronological order from the first time you start thinking about getting elected until election day. At the end there is a summary which can be used as a task list to refer to throughout the campaign.

PART I—PREPARATION

CHAPTER 1

CHOOSING AN OFFICE

The first thing you'll have to do is to choose an office to run for. That may sound easy, but it's really not. You may have dreams of being mayor of your city or of being on the school board, but there are several important things you should consider before calling a press conference and announcing your candidacy.

The first of these is: "How feasible is it for you to win?" The most important factor to consider is whether the incumbent in the office you want plans to run again. If so, be aware that it is very difficult to defeat an incumbent. Most new officeholders are either appointed to fill out an unexpired term or beat out another novice. Just look at the next election for Congress. If there is an incumbent, the seat will usually be considered "safe" and no serious challenger will come forward. So if you can, try to find an office where the incumbent isn't running for re-election.

Another consideration is the political climate. If you want to run for an office that is partisan, (i.e., you must run in a political primary before the election) find out if one party predominates. That is, your area may have an overwhelming majority of one political party or the other. You may be a very well-qualified candidate with no chance of victory if you choose the wrong party. Now, I'm not suggesting that you not be true to your own party preferences, only that you should do some homework and find out. If it doesn't make much difference anyway to you, pick the majority party.

If you just can't stand the party in power, consider a position that is non-partisan. Many local city offices—like school board or city council—fall into this category. You do not declare a party in these races. There may be a primary, but it's just too narrow the field.

Be sure if you do win such a non-partisan election that you avoid getting a political label afterwards—especially the wrong one. For instance, if you become identified with a party, it may work against you on a re-election bid. A shrewd opponent will find ways to let people know your party allegiance—especially if that party is in the minority.

You also should consider carefully if you really want to be elected to the office you have dreamed about. The title of mayor may sound good, but once in the position, you may find out that you don't like to do the work. There's an old saying something like: "Don't wish too hard for something to happen, because it just might come true."

Now, find out where meetings are held for the position you are interested in and attend regularly. Observe carefully and take notes. While in the meeting, ask yourself if you'd like to do the work of a councilman. I know I didn't fully understand what the "nuts and the bolts" of the county board would be. I found that most of the work is dealing with routine matters—like whether we should accept the bid on a new copier in the Law and Justice Center. The press naturally does not report these kinds of activities; so if you just rely on the newspaper for information about the position, you'll only read about the exciting items—which can sometimes be few and far between. This leads into my next suggestion. Follow the position in the media.

In spite of the fact that only the most interesting material is reported, much information about the position can be found in the news media. There is usually a special place in the newspaper for political news and a certain time on the TV and radio news programs for political reports. If you're not watching for them, you may not even be aware of such reporting. I know that, before I got interested in local politics, I was hardly aware of such reports. However, these reports are watched closely by the officeholders themselves and groups in the community that have a stake in the political game. You can be sure that the real estate developers go over zoning case stories with a "fine tooth comb." The point is, you can pick up a lot of information about the position that way. A side benefit will be that you'll already have a lot of information if you do decide to run for the position. At this point, you'll want to know about the issues. More of that later.

If you're still interested in the position, the next step is to do some in-depth research. Your local library is the most logical starting place. There is a wealth of information written about all aspects of political science. Use the index in the library and locate books, magazine articles or newspaper accounts about the job you are interested in. If you have trouble finding material, ask the library staff to help you out. You'd be surprised how helpful they can be if you only ask. What I'm saying is, take the time to learn more about the office before you decide to run. It will be time well spent.

Another good source of information is officeholders in the position you want or in a similar office. If you are afraid of tipping your hand to an incumbent by speaking to people locally, find out the names of officeholders in the next town. Call and ask them to meet for lunch to discuss the office. They probably will be flattered that you asked. Ask what they like and dislike about the job. Ask them about tips for running for the position. Make careful notes after you speak to them.

Now that you've done your homework about the office you want to run for, before you make the decision to run, I recommend you think about the effects of being in office on your family. Sit down and talk to your wife or husband and children about how they feel about your running for office. Without their support, you may have a hard time keeping your spirits up in a political rally while you are worrying about how you're going to have to pay your divorce lawyer or your child's therapist.

A wise politician once told me, "If you want to get your wife's or husband's support for your political activities, help her or him be president of something." People will support you if they feel good about themselves. Encourage your family to be all they can be too. It's contagious.

Now if you've weighed all the factors and are still excited about getting started running for office, you need to have a plan to get elected. However, before we get into that, I've included a chapter that includes several suggestions which could save you lots of time and effort in getting elected which many would-be officeholders overlook.

In summary, you should consider the following things when choosing an office to run for:
1. Is it feasible to win?
2. What is the political climate?
3. Do you really want to do the job?
4. What will be the effects on your family?

NOTES

CHAPTER 2

SHORTCUTS TO OFFICE

Don't be proud. You don't always have to be elected to get into office. Consider these two ways to elected office.

Many a political officeholder first got into office by being appointed to fill an unexpired term. Don't overlook this as a way of getting into office. Keep you eyes and ears open for resignations or deaths of officeholders. There usually is a procedure for applying for the opening. In most instances, the political entity itself (for instance, the city council) will pick a replacement. In a partisan position, the party leadership will often pick the candidate for the next election. If you fail to apply for the job with both the party and the political entity you may find yourself running against the newly appointed incumbent. When I first got on the county board, I was appointed by the county board chairman to fill an unexpired term and then was selected by a caucus of the precinct committeemen to be the candidate in the upcoming election which was several months away. Only one other person applied with the county for the position. Several inquired about the candidate selection, but failed to show up at the political caucus called by the county chairman. In the two subsequent elections I was unopposed. Once you're an incumbent you'll have an advantage in the next election. In fact, many consider incumbency the number one advantage. Most elections for Congress are considered "safe" for the incumbent and most times no viable candidate even applies.

Another shortcut is quite simple. Visit with the incumbent and see if you can persuade him or her to either resign (see above) or to not run again. When I first heard someone suggest this tactic, I thought he was crazy. I thought: "Wouldn't this just tip your hand and give the incumbent a chance to prepare a better campaign?" It might, but in many cases, the incumbent holds on to an office well beyond the point that it is exciting to him or her. He or she does it because nothing better to do has come along. Faced with the prospects of a challenge, he or she often will avoid the fight. It just isn't worth it to him or her.

The best strategy for you is to visit with the incumbent directly and let him or her know you are running for the office. Tell him or her that you plan to run very hard for the position and that you are excited about it. Ask what he or she thinks about it. Depending on the answer, you might want to suggest the incumbent resign now to make it possible for you to get appointed or that he or she withdraw from the race. Ask for his or her help. Thank him or her for any advice. Be understanding to the possible need for the incumbent to find a way to gracefully bow out of the race. Discuss ways in which you could help him or her do this in such a way that the person can save face. If the present officeholder is not interested in your suggestion, be polite and say you are looking forward to running against him or her. This approach may seem overly assertive, but it may save you a lot of effort.

However, if neither of these shortcuts is possible for you, a plan of action is appropriate. The following chapters will outline such a plan. Good luck!

In summary, you should consider two shortcuts to elected office:

1. Be appointed to fill an unexpired term.
2. Convince the incumbent to retire.

NOTES

CHAPTER 3

PUTTING ON YOUR BEST FACE

Before you start setting up a formal campaign committee you need to be sure that you are "ready" to run. That is, you are mentally and physically prepared. A fighter would never consider going into the ring without months of training. Likewise, a fireman would never go into a burning building before he or she had spent months learning about how fires burn and how best to fight them. However, I once met a "would-be" candidate who tossed his hat into the ring but was too scared to call a press conference to announce his candidacy. During the campaign is no time to learn the skills of politics.

First, take the time to assess your own personal strengths and weaknesses. For example: Are you a good speaker? Are you overweight? Do you understand the "art" of politics? Do you like to meet people? Do people like you? Most people, if they are honest, can do a pretty good job of self-assessment. Once you've done that, then establish a personal plan of self-improvement. The intensity of the plan may depend on how difficult it will be to get elected. For example, if you are running for the mayor of New York you'd better train like Rocky in the movie *Rocky* and get the "eye of the tiger." That is, a determination to move mountains, if needed, to achieve your goal. Following are some suggestions you might consider.

Public speaking is one of the weakest areas for most candidates. You may want to concentrate more on this area if the position you are running for requires lots of public speaking. For example, a candidate for mayor will be expected to speak before business groups and, in larger cities, be required to face the press at press conferences. There are several public speaking programs like the *Dale Carnegie Course®* in *Effective Speaking and Human Relations* or speaking clubs like *Toastmasters*. Check around in your area for such programs.

If you don't want to get involved in a formal public speaking program, the common sense rule is that the more you speak in front of groups, the better you will be. I once participated in a mock press conference for a rookie candidate for Sheriff. The campaign committee acted as reporters and we asked as many difficult questions as we could. After several such sessions, our candidate gained a great deal of confidence and performed well in the first live appearance. Even the top candidates spend time practicing. Don't overlook this as part of your strategy.

Another factor to consider is your overall health. When you're campaigning, be at you best. You will be attending many functions and walking door-to-door. The stress will be great. Start a regular program of exercise with the advice of your doctor. If you are overweight, shed those excess pounds—again, with the advice of your doctor.

Appearance is another important factor. Do you have long hair? Do you have a beard? Do you have a ring in your ear(s)—or your nose? I don't mean to offend anyone. In fact, I have had long hair and a beard and I never know what my three children or three stepchildren will look like. I only ask that you be realistic. Look at the appearance of the current officeholders. Try to not be too far off that norm. How many male congressmen have rings in their ears? How many have beards? Then ask yourself how much you want to get elected. Before my first campaign, I agonized over my beard before shaving it off. With a beard, however, I probably wouldn't have been elected.

Clothing is also important. Prepare a wardrobe to help you get elected. If you don't have a decent suit, go buy one. Attend political meetings and find out what the officeholders are wearing and plan accordingly. The important thing is that you want to look good but don't want to stand out. A good example was the time that I wore blazer, tie and dress slacks to a county fair. One of my good political friends took me aside and asked that I look at the other politicians to see what they were wearing. The very popular state representative had on a pair of blue jeans and country shirt. I then removed my coat and tie and rolled up my sleeves. Next year—you guessed it—I was dressed in casual clothes. I didn't quite look like a farmer but at least I didn't stick out too much.

If you feel that you need to learn more about the "art" of politics, you've made a good start by buying this book. Reading books is an excellent way to learn the political ropes. If you think you need more information—especially if you will be running for a major political office—go to the library and look up "politics" in the card catalog. See Appendix 1 for a list of books that I have found helpful.

Part of "putting on a good face" includes having good looking business cards and a resume. If you don't have a resume and aren't sure how to prepare one, it is a good investment to have it professionally prepared. Look in your Yellow Pages under "Resume Service." A resume printed on a laser printer is best.

Business cards can be handed out to people you meet before and during the campaign. Never miss an opportunity to hand someone your business card. That's an important part of "networking" which I will explore more later on. The resume can be used as a basis for campaign literature. Often the news media or groups like the League of Women's Voters will ask for a resume. Again, have an updated copy of your resume available at all times. You never know when you will need it.

Another must is a good quality black and white glossy photo. It can be used for the local newspaper or for campaign brochure material. Go to a professional and tell him or her how you want to use the photo. A good quality photo can be very important. Smart politicians always have one handy.

Now you're almost ready to start on the actual "nuts-and-bolts" of the campaign. If all this preparation hasn't scared you out of the race, read on. There's more fun ahead. Just a note though: Be gentle on yourself at this point. Campaigns have been won without doing all the things I have and will suggest. You will have to decide how many or how few of the suggestions to use. I am outlining what I believe to be the ideal campaign. In all likelihood, you will "out do" the opponent if you follow just a portion of the book.

In summary, be sure you are ready to run:
1. Assess your strengths and weaknesses.
2. Have good health.
3. Have a good appearance.
4. Have appropriate clothing.
5. Read books on politics.
6. Have good campaign material, such as business cards, resume and a photo.

NOTES

CHAPTER 4

LAYING THE GROUNDWORK

Now that you're trim and fit both physically and mentally, the hard work starts. You must begin to lay the groundwork for your campaign. This is one step you shouldn't take lightly. The best lawyers know that the research phase of a lawsuit will win the case, not a flashy courtroom appearance. How does that concept apply, here? In a word, the answer is "preparation."

The truth is that to run a successful campaign you need help. Sometimes lots of it. I have known candidates running campaigns by themselves and forcing their children to pass out brochures. This will work if you have many compliant children or no opponent, but it is usually better to have more help. I have talked with many candidates who see the task of getting people to help as the hardest. They say: "How do you get people to help? I don't know who to ask." Although getting help seems to be hard, in reality it is fairly easy and fun at the same time. It just takes a plan and some old-fashioned work.

Start by getting lists of people in your community. All political entities have lists of their members along with home addresses and phone numbers. Call city hall or the court house and ask. Get lists of community leaders from the Chamber of Commerce. Call the county political chairman of your party and get a list of precinct committeemen and lists of members of political clubs. Note the officers. Find out where they meet. Get lists of members of social clubs such as Kiwanis or the Lions. As you meet people day-to-day, ask for their names and addresses. Take an interest in people. Put all the names you can on a list. Include friends and associates. It should be easy to compile a list of several hundred names.

Next, establish a calendar of events for yourself. Mark down dates for meetings of political clubs, "official" political meetings, like school board meetings, or social events you can find. You might want to focus on events that relate to the race. For example, if you are running for the school board, you might attend school ice cream socials, sport booster events or PTA meetings.

Then, start attending these events. The point is to meet lots of people. *Become known*. It is a good idea to keep a few index cards in your pocket and, as you meet someone new, record on the card the name and any other information you can learn about the person. Now, don't just pull the card out as you are talking and be obvious. You may offend some. Rather, as you are leaving the room or are alone, record what you know. Also, you can fill in the address and phone number the next day from the phone book. It is not important at this stage to tell the people you meet directly about your political ambitions, but if the subject comes up naturally and they volunteer to help, record this also on the index card.

Just a note: Use your common sense about what events to attend. Only attend events in the geographic area for the office you want or be sure the events will have people attending from your area. I worked for a town council candidate who attended a Penn State Club Alumni party being held locally only to find out that only two members were from the town where the election was being held. Her time was wasted. (Except the party was great.) A simple question to the club president (me) would have prevented this error or at least have given the candidate the choice not to attend.

If another political campaign is going on, volunteer to help. Get to know people in that campaign. Record names of people you meet on index cards. As a side benefit, you may get some ideas for your own campaign by working for someone else.

Also, consider becoming more active in your local political party organization. Call the party chairman and volunteer to help. There are always many opportunities available. Don't feel you have to do everything. Do things you would enjoy. Also, where I lived, by donating $100.00 a year, you became a "sustaining member" of the local party and were entitled to attend several events free as well as receive the party newsletter. As you become more active, as a party "regular," you can meet many people who may help with your campaign. I also found that these people were very friendly, honest and willing to support people interested in running for office. It just makes sense to build these positive relationships early.

Just a note: Don't become active in any organization just to gain political support. People will know that and resent your self-serving involvement. Do it because you enjoy it and try to be helpful to others. However, be honest about your ambitions and if people volunteer to help, make note of their offer.

But where am I going here? It's simple. You want names of people-lots of them. These names will serve as a pool of possibilities to help you in your campaign. At a minimum, it will give you names of people who are likely to vote for you once you are running since you will be a person and no longer a name to them. However, at this point, that is just a side benefit. This may sound like a lot of work just to gather names, but it is extremely important. In my community, the most sought after helpers in campaigns had lists of names to call on and they were always keeping them current. I myself had recorded hundreds of names and addresses on index cards of people I had met while attending events or had taken from lists. As my own list increased, I created a data file in my personal computer. I used this data in my own campaigns and for people I was helping.

I knew a candidate for judge who spent over two years attending political social events all over his district. He just went to the event and sat down and talked to people around him. He carried three or four index cards in his pocket at all times. As soon as he left the event, he recorded the name and any other information he had found out in the conversation on the cards. He had a shoe box full of cards by the time I talked to him. Guess who made up his campaign committee team for the campaign? These same people listed on the cards. He had the best organized campaign and won the election easily. Some people thought he was just lucky to win.

But really, I'm ahead of myself a little. You just need to know that these lists of people should be kept handy for future reference. A side benefit will be that you'll make many friends. This is the secret of "networking" that sales people have used for years. The most successful sales people network, know lots of people and sell lots of their products. In this case, the product is you.

By now you are well on your way to having a good campaign started. However, the next step in very critical. Read on.

In summary, you should start laying the groundwork for your campaign.
1. Get lists of people to help.
2. Establish a calendar of events and attend these events.
3. Help in other campaigns.
4. Become a party "regular."

NOTES

CHAPTER 5

CHOOSING A CAMPAIGN MANAGER

By this time, you should be excited. You know what office you want. You are at your best and you have lists of lots of people who can help you get elected. Now you need to step back and pause before you jump into the campaign. Take time to pick a good campaign manager. "But why don't I be my own campaign manager?" you ask. The answer is simple. You must now move into another role—candidate. Being a candidate is a demanding job in itself. You simply can't afford the time to attend to all the minor details of the campaign. Let someone else do it. Did you ever hear the saying that "A lawyer who represents himself has a fool for a client"? How many doctors do you see that treat themselves? This rule also applies in politics. Lay your ego aside and you just may win.

Just a note: I recommend that you not name your spouse as your campaign manager. That could be a bad mistake. He or she is too close to you to do the things that are needed in a campaign. It's hard to keep professional detachment with a spouse. If you argue with your spouse about minor household issues (as I do), can you imagine trying to agree on how to run a political campaign? But enough of this. Just trust me. I've never seen it work.

First, prepare a job write-up. Outline what is expected. For example, job duties might include:
1. coordinating campaign activities,
2. having weekly meetings,
3. reporting to candidate regularly on progress.

Then ask local political leaders for advice about possible candidates for campaign manager. A good place to start is the local county political party chairman. Use your lists to identify these leaders. They will be glad to suggest names of people who would be eager to help. You would be amazed at the number of political "animals" around who just love to be involved in politics. In my old county, the same faces appeared in most political campaigns. These people never wanted to run for an office. They just loved the excitement of a political race—and for no pay. It sounds crazy, but believe me it's true. Then again review the lists of contacts you've made and also consider people you think would be good for the job.

The next step is to sit down and start phoning these potential campaign managers and simply ask them if they are interested. If you get a positive response, start meeting with the people over "coffee" and chat. While you do this, have your job write-up in mind.

When you make a choice, consider these factors. First, who referred the candidate for campaign manager? If the county chairman gave you the name, the person is probably good. Also ask the candidate what experience he or she has had. The more political experience the better—especially if the candidate he or she was helping won.

The last consideration is often overlooked at the local level, but I feel it is still important—balance. What do I mean? Balance the campaign manager with yourself. For example, if you are a single woman, find a married man. If you are a married man, consider a married woman. As I said earlier, never choose a relative, especially a spouse. Why? The balance with yourself gives more appeal to your campaign. Female workers would be more apt to help a male candidate with a female campaign manager. Without the balance—if for example, both the campaign manager and the candidate for mayor were male—the campaign might be considered a "male-dominated race." The same principle is used in national elections to select candidates for president and vice-president, but usually the balance in that case is by the region of the country. But again, please trust me. These seem to be the unwritten rules of the game that work the best.

The final step is to select the one person from those you've talked to run your campaign. Once you make the selection, be sure to tell that person how valuable he or she is to the campaign and that you expect much. Good politicians have found that the more you ask for, the more you'll get. People like to feel needed and valuable.

Good luck. Things should be beginning to "heat up." The rest of the book will be valuable to both you and the campaign manager and should be read as advice to both of you. I would, however, ask him or her to go back and read the whole book.

In summary, you now need to choose a campaign manager.
1. It is important to have one.
2. Don't choose your spouse.
3. Prepare a job write-up.
4. Ask local political leaders for advice.
5. Pick someone who will add "balance" to the campaign.
6. Make a selection.

NOTES

CHAPTER 6

GETTING STARTED

Now that you have a campaign manager, you can start getting your campaign under way. The two of you should sit down and review the lists of names you have collected and start to select people to ask to be on your committee. Pick a very few people at first. People you can trust—whom you can work with. Go in with a positive attitude that people will be willing to help. Your attitude *will* make a difference. Call the people or better still, pay them a personal visit. I almost always helped in a campaign if the candidate made the effort to ask me personally. I was flattered. Again, tell them their presence in your campaign is very important, and that you need their help. You can't get elected without the help and support of people. You need these people more than they need you. Be humble and honest.

Then, schedule your first campaign meeting right away for a strategy session which should include a select group of campaign workers. Your house or the campaign manager's house would be OK. Serve coffee and light snacks and keep it informal. At the first meeting, just discuss general strategy and get to know each other. During the meeting, review the list of potential helpers and identify others to be called later.

One important thing to accomplish early in the campaign is to appoint someone treasurer. Assign this person the job of studying the laws concerning disclosure of campaign funds and political contributions, if he or she is not already familiar with these laws. If you are lucky, a CPA or lawyer will volunteer and do an excellent job. Have a bank account set up to deposit monies.

The next item would be to appoint someone to go to the courthouse or local government office to get the petitions necessary to have your name placed on the ballot. You will have to get a certain number of signatures on the petition to get on the ballot. Some elections will have a primary before the general election. That is done to narrow the field of candidates in a non-partisan election or to select the party candidate in a partisan election.

At one of your early organizing meetings, pass out petitions to the members of your committee and ask them to help you gather names. It is also important that you gather names too. The more people you meet, the more support you will get. The signers must be registered voters in the district in which you are voting and the signatures and addresses must match the voting registration records exactly. The specific instructions for completing the petitions usually will be included when you pick them up. Check your state's election laws to be certain you are completing the petitions properly.

The petitions will be verified by the election officials and can even be challenged by your opponent. I have known some campaign committees that focused on the petitions of the other candidate—hoping for a disqualification and an easy victory for their candidate. However, I wouldn't recommend that as a campaign strategy. Running a good positive campaign is the best way to insure victory.

Plan to get at least twice as many names on the petitions as you need—more if possible. There are several reasons for this. First, in the event someone challenges your candidacy, the names will be checked. Some may be invalidated because the signers are not registered or do not live in the district. The second reason is that you should keep the names and addresses of the signers for future use. These people should be considered your "supporters" now and should be solicited for help in the campaign and also should be reminded to vote for you near the election. These names should be treated as a valuable resource. The final reason is that a large number of names on the petitions is a show of strength and support for your candidacy. It is also a good idea to let the news media know how many people signed your petitions. By doing this, you may create the "bandwagon effect" which will motivate even more people to support you. Many people want to be on the winning side.

Perhaps the most important task for your small committee to accomplish early in the campaign is to announce your candidacy. Work with your campaign manger or someone talented in writing to develop a press release. Keep it as simple as possible. Include the position you are seeking and your name, address and phone number. Also, mention where you work, your educational background, what political experience you have had and some information about your family. You may want to highlight several of your special achievements and list affiliations—like being a member of the Elks. Attach the glossy black and white picture that you had taken earlier. The statement should be typed, double spaced on a single page. Pass copies of this out to all local newspapers and radio stations. If the race is significant, contact the local TV stations too.

You may want to call a press conference to announce your candidacy and to answer questions. However, before you do this—especially if this is you first political race—have a "mock" press conference with your committee as reporters. (See chapter 3.) The most important thing is to remain calm in such situations. You do not need a perfect answer to each question nor do you need to answer each question directly. The most experienced candidates will prepare a list of answers to possible questions that put their candidacy in the best light. As questions are asked in the press conference, they give their prepared answers even if the answer is only remotely related to the question. The technique of "bridging" is helpful to accomplish this. For example, if you are asked what your position is on budget deficits you might say:

"That is a good question. I feel strongly about deficits. Especially when it impacts on the quality of education. Teachers should only be hired if they have a master's degree. Our children deserve no less."

Note that the question was not answered. Nowhere in the rules does it say you have to answer someone else's question. Use the press conference to achieve your own goals—that is, to put yourself in the best light. Watch a press conference at the national level to see how this works.

It's a very good idea to prepare a letter to be sent to your closest friends and associates to announce your candidacy. Use the lists you previously made for the names. Tell why you are running. Then simply ask for help. Have a tear-off section at the end which has a place for name, address and phone number and boxes to check off for helping like:

- ☐ I will help passing out literature.
- ☐ I will put out a yard sign.
- ☐ I will contribute $ _____ which is enclosed.
- ☐ I will send a letter to the editor.
- ☐ I will host a coffee to meet the candidate.

Ask that the slip be returned. Never ask for help in a general way. This may scare people away. Make the tasks simple. You will find that people will volunteer for a small task, and once they do that, they will volunteer to do more. That was how I usually got involved in a campaign. I was taught this in an excellent seminar I attended for Penn State club leaders. One speaker pointed out that it is human nature to be hesitant to attempt a large task, but most people will agree to do a small task.

Try to send out at least 200 letters. Many people will return the slips. Appoint someone to handle coordinating sending out the letters and handling the returns. If possible, find someone with a micro-computer who can create a data file to keep track of the information marked on the slips. This data can be used later to create reports for people organizing campaign activities. Excellent computer programs such as Q & A or PFS: Professional File used with PFS: Professional Write are available which will also allow you to merge form letters with your address lists. Save the slips you get back for future use. You should also get some money returned to start your campaign war chest. Your treasurer should deposit the checks in your campaign account immediately and take note of information that needs to be reported under campaign disclosure laws.

Now, you should be started and be ready to get more organized. But first remember, you are now a candidate. Start wearing a large name tag wherever you go. Don't miss any opportunity to introduce yourself or to pass out a business card. Get yourself into a campaign mentality. Get your campaign committee to start wearing a button with your name on it. This will start a positive campaign mentality which will grow. Read on.

In summary, you are ready to get your campaign started.
1. Pick a very few people to help at first.
2. Schedule a campaign meeting.
3. Appoint someone treasurer.
4. File petitions.
5. Announce your candidacy.
6. Hold a press conference.
7. Send an announcement letter.

NOTES

CHAPTER 7

BUILDING THE CAMPAIGN ORGANIZATION

The next step is to build a more formal campaign organization. Up to now, you have been working with a small group or "inner circle" and your campaign manager. This step is just expanding on that since more things have to be done. Start delegating as much as you can to other people and let your campaign manager handle the day-to-day details. The campaign manager should start contacting more people to help. Again, use the names of people you collected while you were laying the groundwork and networking. Also, use the names from your petitions and from the tear-off slips in your announcement letter.

As I said before, "political animals" in the area will probably contact you to volunteer—especially if your campaign has had some publicity There are always people "out there" who love politics. I know, because I am one of them. These people can be your best workers. Let **them** tell you how **they** can help. This is an important thing to do for all your helpers. The campaign can be fun if people are free to use their God-given talents as they see fit.

You or your campaign manager will need to appoint more people to head up important jobs. Again, I recommend that you be sure to tell the people that you appoint that their jobs are important. Different jobs to consider might be publicity, finance, recruitment and training of volunteers, newsletter editor, voter registration and volunteer activities coordinator. Discuss what other jobs are needed with your committee. The important thing here is to get excitement in your campaign. People get more excited if they feel what they are doing is important. Create lots of jobs and titles. Then, when brochures must be passed out, your "Department Heads" will be the first in line to volunteer. Also, don't forget to send thank-you notes throughout the campaign. A little appreciation will go a long way.

Just a note here: Don't worry too much about the qualifications of your top people. Look for people who are eager to do the work and are excited about your candidacy. I once got my top job as county newsletter editor by mentioning to someone at a political meeting that I enjoyed doing newsletters. The person I was talking to told the party chairman and in five minutes I had the job. The point is that you are getting free help and should not pass up an offer of help. That is, unless you are wealthy and can afford to hire professionals. In that case, you probably won't need this book either. Seriously, in some situations, I've even seen "co-chairman" of committees named because two people wanted the same job.

Building The Campaign Organization

As you build a bigger committee and become more organized, start to hold regular meetings. Pick a time and a day and stick to that each week. Seven P.M. often works well in the middle of the week. Keep the business agenda light for the first few meetings. Let people get to know each other. Serve coffee and cookies or other snacks and make your campaign an important social event.

Before the regular meeting, plan an agenda of what you need to get accomplished. Also, leave some time to brainstorm. Let your campaign manager run the meetings but be sure everyone on the committee is encouraged to participate and make decisions. Don't forget to make the meetings a social event that people will want to attend. Your success in the election will depend on an active and strong committee.

However, before you get too far along with the campaign, step back and develop a strategy for the campaign. This could be critical.

In summary, a campaign organization should be built.
1. Find people who love politics to help.
2. Appoint department heads.
3. Have regular meetings.
4. Plan an agenda for the meetings.

NOTES

CHAPTER 8

STRATEGY

One task that your new committee should tackle early is to plan a good strategy for your campaign. I feel this is so important that I am devoting a separate chapter to this subject. Developing a strategy is an area of politics that is definitely an art and not a science.

The first and perhaps the most important step of this campaign phase is to develop a theme for the campaign that fits the particular situation of the candidate. For example, if you are running against an incumbent, "Time for a Change" might be appropriate. If you are the incumbent, "Experience Counts" would be a good theme. A good way to develop a theme is to analyze your opponent's weaknesses in relationship to your strengths. For example, I worked in a campaign where some people felt that the opponent was not a good manager of money. Our candidate was an auditor. The theme I suggested was: "A Candidate You Can Trust." We then structured our advertising around this theme and built a case to show the voters why they could trust our candidate. We never directly said that the opponent couldn't be trusted, but people got the idea anyway. In fact, the theme reinforced the perception that some people had of our opponent. It is hard to run against such a well thought out theme since to counteract it you would have to constantly be defending your weakness and not emphasizing your strengths. I used this method once myself when I was running for precinct committeeman against an incumbent. I found out that the incumbent was not very active and did not help the party by passing out literature or other activities. My theme was "A Precinct Committeeman Who Will Work for The Party." The theme had the subtle message that my opponent didn't work for the party. When I visited with people walking door-to-door, I often asked: "Have you ever met the current Precinct Committeeman?" The answer was almost always "no," to which I replied: "I promise if I am elected that you will get to know me."

Richard Nixon won the 1968 campaign for the Presidency with the theme "Law and Order." This played into the fears people had with the ghetto riots of the early sixties and the perception that the Democrat President Lyndon Johnson had not handled the situation well. The perception of Johnson's weakness rubbed off on Hubert Humphrey and Nixon's theme took advantage of the Democrat's weakness. Nixon was a master at this strategy.

Once you have selected the theme, keep it in mind in all phases of the campaign. Use it in your literature, your speeches, your press releases and keep it in mind as you visit with people about your campaign.

In fact, I strongly recommend that in this stage of your preparations—while you are developing your strategy and theme—that you work with your inner circle to develop a brochure. It should feature the theme on the first page and include a picture of yourself. Keep the brochure simple—one page, both sides would be adequate. Include your qualifications and a short paragraph about what you will do if elected. Review the issues that you researched earlier for ideas. (See chapter one.) Keep in mind what was discussed about the theme by your committee. Highlight positive features. Print several hundred copies for early in the campaign but plan to revise as the campaign progresses. If you can find a professional advertising person or copywriter to help, do so. Make your brochure simple and neat and be sure your name is featured often and prominently.

Another consideration in your strategy is to be sure you are emphasizing your strengths. For example, if you don't look like Robert Redford or Julia Roberts, but speak well, have lots of radio advertising. If you have a good-looking family, be sure to use their pictures in your brochure. The key here is to use common sense.

Sometimes it can be helpful to add things to your strategy that are unexpected. The first campaign I worked in was during my college days at Penn State. Our candidate for student body president was an unknown commodity running against the popular president of the junior class. The committee created tiny stickers with the words "Who's Berkowitz" on them and stuck them up all over campus months before the campaign started. Before long, people were going crazy trying to find out who Berkowitz was and what he would be doing. We never told them, but the stickers kept on getting bigger until we called a press conference to tell everyone who Berkowitz was. The campaign was off to a great start and our problem of name recognition was easily overcome with a very small outlay of money.

A caution is in order here. When developing your strategy, be careful you don't oversell yourself. This is a judgment call, but I have seen campaigns where the candidate's face and name were "plastered" all over town. People were deluged with literature and phone calls. The result was that people were "turned off" and voted against the candidate. Sales people know that a product can be over sold. Don't be caught in this trap.

Related to this, is timing of the campaign. Be sure that you don't "peak" early. That is, don't concentrate on an activity like advertising early in the campaign. You need to have the maximum popularity on election day. Also, if you are planning to have a brochure passed out door-to-door, you might want to wait till later in the campaign. (See chapter 10.) People have a tendency to forget. Be sure they don't forget your candidate. Door-to-door campaigning by the candidate on a personal basis early in the campaign followed by an extensive mailing or passing out of a brochure later in the campaign is a good strategy. The brochure reinforces the initial contact. But again be sure that you don't oversell. One brochure is enough.

Once you have a strategy planned, you should start your campaign activities in earnest. You are almost elected!

In summary, before you start your campaign activities, plan a strategy for your campaign.
1. Develop a theme.
2. Create a brochure or hand-out.
3. Emphasize your strengths.
4. Add the unexpected.
5. Don't oversell.
6. Consider timing of the campaign.

NOTES

PART II—THE CAMPAIGN

CHAPTER 9

EARLY CAMPAIGN ACTIVITIES

By this time, you have your campaign well under way. Your petitions have been filed; you have a campaign manager and a committee; you have announced your candidacy and you have your strategy in mind. Most important, you look and act like a candidate. Now is the time to start working on campaign activities.

For simplicity, I have broken the campaign into three phases:

1. Early campaign activities,
2. Middle campaign activities, and
3. Final campaign activities/the countdown.

Each of these phases is covered in a separate chapter. Just a note: Use the information you gathered from your "tear off letter" (see chapter 6) to recruit people for these activities.

In this chapter, we will explore the following early campaign activities:

1. Fund raisers
2. Attending meetings and events
3. Establishing a newsletter
4. Door-to-door campaigning

You should probably start planning a fund raiser at this point. Your tear-off letter should have generated some funds, but you will need more. A fund raiser early in the campaign is the best idea. Trying to raise money late in the campaign may be difficult since by this time the potential givers may have been invited and have attended fund raisers for other candidates. Also, if you plan to have a fund raiser after the election, forget it. People usually won't be interested after the election—win or lose. I know a judicial candidate who waited till after the election to have a fund raiser to pay off campaign debts. Guess what? He had to dip into his own pocket heavily to pay off the debts.

I believe that the best fund raisers are simple. That is, you don't need fancy food or entertainment. Hot dogs and chips with soda pop are fine. Try to find a local band to perform for free. Pick a date and have lots of tickets printed. Again, try to find a printer to donate the printing. I don't know why, but it seems the more tickets you print, the more you sell. There must be some psychological principle at work.

Give each member of your committee a stack of tickets and ask each one to sell at least ten tickets. Charge a reasonable amount. It seems that when you start charging more than it would take someone to go out for dinner at a nice restaurant, people will stay away. A

$10.00 donation each seemed to work well in the campaigns I have been involved in. A good strategy is to have people sell tickets to groups that like to network—like real estate agents. The largest fund raiser I ever helped organize was successful because we had several real estate agents selling to other agents. Remember that sales people love to attend events where people will be. Also, they are great at selling tickets and they enjoy it. A side benefit is that most successful sales people genuinely like people and are fun to have on a campaign.

If you are a professional, be sure to have someone selling to your professional group. Lawyers will support other lawyers. The same goes for teachers and other professionals. In the campaign for Judge mentioned earlier, we sold a great many tickets to lawyers.

Another good strategy is to create a letter of invitation to the fund raiser to be sent out to lists of people involved in politics—like precinct committeemen or members of political clubs. Have the letter signed by the local chairman of the political party if you can. Put it on your candidate's letterhead. Enclose five or more tickets for the person to sell and tell the seller they can have one free for his or her help. This sounds like you would have a lot of "free-loaders" at the event, but the person who uses a free ticket will often bring someone and pay for their ticket. Also, people are more apt to sell tickets if they attend. I got lots of free tickets this way, but I always sold many tickets too. Don't forget to send free tickets to other candidates if they will attend. Also, advertise that other political candidates will be there too. Make this an important political event!

The day of the event, have several members of your committee assigned to collect tickets and money at the door. Never turn anyone away who forgot to buy a ticket in advance. That is another reason why simple fund raisers are a good idea. If too many people show up, you can always run out an buy extra hot dogs and soda.

As you were laying the groundwork for your campaign, you should have been attending social- and club-type functions. (See chapter 4.) This activity should be continued during the campaign and even increased. If fact, you should also be looking for opportunities to speak to these groups too. It is a good idea to assign someone to keep a calendar for you and remind you when these events take place. Ask people on your committee to watch out for opportunities for you to attend and/or speak at events. There will be people on your committee in Kiwanis, the Elks, PTA's, the Rotary etc., etc. I found that a committee could find enough events to keep the candidate busy until the end of the campaign. You should always wear your name tag at these events and take an ample supply of your brochures. If possible, put the brochures on the tables in front of where people will be sitting before the program starts. Also, be sure you attend as many political events as possible—especially political committee meetings for your party. One place where I lived had a monthly Republican Precinct Committeeman Breakfast that was also attended by officials and candidates. Believe me, it was noticed when a candidate didn't show up. The people who attended the breakfast were the influential people in the party who knew lots of people. Their opinion counted.

Another worthwhile activity is to establish a campaign newsletter. It is a good idea to give this project to just one person. Mail it to all your supporters and to campaign workers. It should include information on upcoming events and a calendar of these events. Information about the candidate and his or her activities should also be included. It is a good way to thank people who are helping also. Feature stories about the key people in your campaign committee. Include lots of praise. You may even get some volunteers for your committee from the supporters who read the newsletter. You can also include a tear-off coupon for donations or for volunteering to help similar to the one you used in your campaign letter earlier in the campaign.

Another campaign activity that you should start early is door-to-door campaigning. This is an activity that is best done by the candidate and it can never be started too early. You should knock at the door or ring the doorbell and, when someone answers, introduce yourself and explain that you are running for office. Always leave your campaign brochure—even if the person isn't home. (Carry a pocket of rubber bands for this. They work great for holding brochures on door knobs.) Ask if the person has any questions for you or if you can be of help in any way. There is no need to give a big speech or stay too long. Listen carefully to what the people say. You can find out a lot this way. Take index cards with you and record names and information. If the person wants to help with your campaign, mark this down. Also, note if they promise to vote for you. You should be sure a call is made to this person right before the election to reinforce this promise. Treat each person and his or her vote as special.

The purpose for such visits is three-fold. First, you want these people to vote for you. Next, you want help if they offer it. Lastly, you want to develop confidence in meeting people and to gain momentum for your campaign. There is no better way than door-to-door campaigning. It's a sure way to get off on an excellent start. Most candidates I know who did this won, and mostly won big. In fact, one relatively unknown candidate for town council whom I knew visited almost every home in town and easily led a large field of candidates. Remember this: If you meet someone face-to-face and they promise to support you, in most cases, you will have that person's vote for as many times as you run and even for different offices. A very successful state representative shared that secret with me. He considered this activity so special and important that he walked door-to-door in every campaign—even if he was unopposed. Serious sales people will tell you that the best way to sell—and that's what politics is all about—is to put yourself before people and ask them for something. In this case, it's their vote.

Where should you walk? Some candidates get lists of people who voted in the last primary for the candidate's political party and only visit these people. If you have up-to-date and accurate lists, this may be a good strategy. In effect, you are focusing your energies on voters who vote every time. This is an efficient way to campaign since you are not spending valuable time visiting people who in all probability will not vote. Also, if you are aware of areas where people tend to vote heavily, be sure to walk in these areas. County records will show the percent of voter turn-out.

In my race for precinct committeeman, I used a list of Republican voters that was sorted by street address. I visited each and every house on the list—even if I had to come back several times to meet the people.

However, if you have the time, I recommend that you walk entire neighborhoods and meet everybody. Word will spread that you've been around and you may even sway a few people from the other party to vote for you. Remember that each vote is special. I strongly recommend that the candidate keep going door-to-door throughout the campaign—even if it is only for a few hours a week later in the campaign.

Your campaign committee should be meeting regularly now. Once a week should be sufficient. Plan the meeting for the same day and time to make it easy for people to mark their calendars. Keep up the good work. You're almost elected!

In summary, you should consider the following early campaign activities that were introduced in this chapter:

1. Having a fund raiser
2. Attending meetings and events
3. Establishing a newsletter
4. Starting door-to-door campaigning

NOTES

CHAPTER 10

MIDDLE CAMPAIGN ACTIVITIES

By this time, you are about halfway into your planned campaign. In this chapter, we will explore the following middle campaign activities:

1. Coffees
2. Advertising
   a. Yard signs
   b. Letters to The Editor
   c. Endorsements
   d. Brochures
   e. Newspaper ads
   f. Radio and TV ads
3. Voter registration drives
4. Letters to groups

Having "coffees" are a good way to let people meet the candidate. I recommend starting this activity in the middle of the campaign since you can easily ask your well-established committee members and people you've met during the campaign to host a coffee. However, if you prefer, you could start this activity earlier.

A "coffee" is a party hosted by a supporter in a neighborhood so that people can meet the candidate. The coffee is a good way to really get to know people and to let them really get to know you. First, you have to find someone to sponsor a coffee. (Ask your committee members or check your "lists.") You ask the person to pick a night on which you can visit his or her home. Ask this host to invite friends and neighbors. Suggest that he or she send out a hand-written postcard and that it be followed up with a phone call reminder.

The coffee should start around 7 P.M. and it would be appropriate to serve coffee, tea and desert. The coffee doesn't have to be fancy, just a friendly atmosphere is all that's needed. Take your brochures with you and some 3x5 index cards. You don't need to make a big speech at the coffee. Just introduce yourself, give a brief overview of your qualifications and ask for questions. If you don't know all the answers, that's OK. Follow up later personally with a phone call. That gives you the opportunity to make an even better impression.

A coffee should be short. One or two hours would be sufficient. While you are there, record names, addresses and phone numbers of people who want to help with your campaign. Don't be shy about asking for support and for help. Many good volunteers can be recruited this way.

I feel that advertising is something that should not be started too early in the campaign and I consider it an activity that also should start in earnest about mid-campaign. As I mentioned earlier, you don't want to over-sell yourself or peak too early. Several of the campaigns I worked on timed advertising to peak several weeks before election day. Following are some advertising ideas.

One good (and free) way to advertise is to place yard signs that advertise your campaign. Put someone in charge of this activity. Ask people on the committee to sign up for yard signs. Look through your lists for possibilities for signs. The more you can put out the better. I worked on a campaign for judge where people in the community were actually counting the number of signs. People considered the candidate with the most signs the "leader" and many people want to vote for the winner. It's the old "band wagon" philosophy. That is an unfortunate reality in politics and you have to be aware of that fact. You have to act like a winner and lots of signs is a good way to do that.

You will have to check local zoning laws to find out when you can put signs out, placement of signs and size restrictions. I recommend you start this activity as soon as you legally can and keep the signs up throughout the campaign. Signs are especially critical for a new unknown candidate. They help with the name recognition problem and show the public that you are a serious candidate.

It is usually better to have professionally made signs that will look good and hold up outside under all weather conditions. Check the Yellow Pages in your phone directory under "Signs" or "Advertising Specialties."

Get names of people who are willing to put out signs. Be sure you tell people that your committee will place the signs (with permission) and remove them after the campaign. There are several reasons for this. First, if you place the signs you can be sure they comply with local codes. Second, people may "say" they will put out a sign if you give it to them, but actually will not follow through and put one out. As a side note: I knew a local political party chairman who insisted that follow-though was the most important thing to consider in a campaign. He urged that the committee follow up on every activity to be sure that it was actually being done. He urged that it be done in a positive way, but believed that without follow-up most tasks would go undone. I tend to trust people; however, I think that this is probably good advice.

Another thing to consider is that people are more apt to agree to a yard sign if you do all the work. Be sure you remove the sign promptly after the campaign since you may want to use that yard again. Also, be sure your workers do not damage the yard or shrubs.

Target key locations such as on a busy street or highway or heavily travelled corners. Especially look for places near businesses and workplaces. Also try to find commercial locations where you can put signs. Sometimes, business people have vacant lots where you can put up large signs that comply with sign codes. Ask people on your committee if they know anybody with such a vacant lot.

Remember, don't be shy. You need to get your message across and create a winning psychology. Signs are an excellent way to do this. In one campaign I worked on, in a town I had just moved in to, I was told there was an "informal gentleman's agreement" to not put out signs because they were "unsightly." However, I still recommended that signs be put out. The period the signs are out is minimal—a month or so—and the effect can be critical to the campaign. In fact, the "ban" was recommended in this case by the incumbents who wouldn't benefit as much by signs. I also feel there are first amendment constitutional rights involved and local authorities can not legally ban signs—although they can impose "reasonable" restrictions such as size and location. In one town, signs could not be put next to the curb.

Also, don't just put up the signs and forget about them. Have someone follow-up on the signs that are taken down or disappear (believe me they will!) and replace them. College students love to steal signs as "souvenirs." Also your opponent's overzealous supporters may take the signs down. In one hotly contested judge race, the signs had to be replaced almost every two days. In fact, that worked to our advantage because people started commenting about our determination.

Another free way to advertise is by sending letters to the editors of the local papers. This, again, should not be started too early in the campaign. People have a tendency to "forget." Most papers will gladly publish the letters since they generate great interest. If you think that political letters are spontaneous, you are mistaken. Many campaigns will have people assigned to work on this activity. They will actually "ghost-write" the letters and find someone to sign them. If you choose to do this, have the letters typed and be sure the people actually read and sign the letters. The newspaper will follow up and check this out.

Address the letters to the editor and add a complete address and phone number. Sometimes it will speed up the process if the letters are hand-delivered and the verification done right in the newspaper's office. If someone wants to write their own letter, that is OK, but ask him or her if you can review the letter before it is sent.

In general, the letter should be brief and to the point. Lengthy letters usually aren't read or understood. Most people only scan the paper anyway. Reporters know this; so they put the important stuff up front. The focus should be on your strengths and the letter should mention your name often. Letters to the editor will heighten public interest in you as a candidate and surprisingly many people actually tally how each side is doing. It can become like an opinion survey. The candidate with the most letters often wins.

Related to this is getting the endorsement of the local paper, radio or TV stations. This is free advertising too. I have seen studies that show that getting endorsements is one of the most important factors in getting elected. Usually you will be asked to provide a biography or be asked into the editor's office for an interview. Be sure you cooperate fully and put on your best face. If you are not contacted, call the editor and ask for an interview. Be positive about this and try to project a winning attitude. I suspect that sometimes the editor will endorse those that he or she feels will win anyway—to make it seem that the newspaper had an influence on the outcome.

Also, try to get endorsements from unions or other groups. Again, this is free advertising. Never turn down an invitation to address a group and to ask for their support. The League of Women Voters usually holds a debate before each election and the League will not endorse a candidate; however, these debates usually create media interest and are attended by many interested voters. In fact, usually the attendees are influential people who will "spread the word around" about your candidacy. Don't pass up such an invitation.

Paid advertising is also critical to your campaign. Again, I recommend starting this activity in mid-campaign to avoid "peaking" too early.

First, as I mentioned in chapter 8, you should have a good handout or brochure. This may be a good time to rewrite the brochure with the help of your new campaign manager and your now more experienced committee. Use what you've learned so far in the rewrite.

Plan to have the brochure delivered door-to-door by you and your campaign workers. It is best to start increasing this activity at this point in the campaign. As I mentioned before, timing is important. You want to have the greatest support later in the campaign—closer to election day. Again, you may want to consider to whom you pass out the brochure and where you will pass it out. As I alluded to in the last chapter, you can concentrate on people who vote regularly or on areas where people tend to vote more. However, if it is practicable, cover the entire voting area.

Have your workers knock on each door and hand the brochure to the prospective voter. Have them ask for the prospective voter's support on election day. A personal contact like this can not be beat. If the person is not home, a brochure should always be left. Again, have your workers carry rubber bands in their pockets. They work great for attaching brochures to doorknobs. I especially enjoyed working with someone else while passing out literature. I would work one side of the street, while the other person would work the other side. After we were done, we headed for a coffee shop to compare notes.

You should also consider running newspaper ads. Start with a few ads around the middle of the campaign and increase the number and size of the ads closer to election day. These can be expensive and some feel that, for a local race, not very effective for the cost—compared to personal visits. You will have to use your judgement here—especially consider how much you can afford to spend. Include a picture and a very short version of your biography. Be sure your name is in large print and put your number on the ballot in the ad—if you know it. Try to get the ad in the Sunday paper if possible since it is usually the most widely read.

I have worked on campaigns where lists of supporters were made into an ad, This can be effective if you get lots of names. In one campaign, we circulated a sign-up sheet at a campaign function and asked for a small donation to cover the ad. People like to see their name in print and will usually donate for this.

Radio ads, surprisingly, are often cheaper than newspaper ads; so don't overlook this as a possibility. Choose time spots when people are coming and going from work if you have the option to choose. Many stations will sell a package of ads and fit them in where they can over a range of hours. Plan short ads that are read by a professional. Usually someone on the committee knows a current or retired radio announcer who will volunteer his or her time. Try to time these ads close to the election to reinforce other advertising.

TV ads should only be considered for major races since they are relatively expensive. You will want to have your commercials professionally done. This is a tricky media and you should be sure that, if you use it, the commercials are done right. I attended a national convention and sat in on two seminars by a TV media expert who was a former TV newsman. He said the best TV commercials should be less than fifteen seconds and be focused on the visual not verbal. Major political campaigns use TV a lot and hire people who specialize in this media.

Perhaps one of the most important activities that you could start at this point would be a voter registration drive. The goal of the activity would be to be certain that all your supporters are registered to vote. It is a good idea to put someone in charge of this activity.

First, be sure that when you go door-to-door or meet people at events, you ask the people who plan to vote for you if they are registered. You will be surprised at the number of people who will tell you they will support you, but are afraid to admit they are not registered. Keep track of people who need to be registered and follow-up with an offer to help that person get registered.

One way to proceed with a registration drive is to target areas of the city where there has been a lot of growth or new building. Send teams of people door-to-door and have them ask the people if they are registered to vote. Have the team members tell the people that they are a part of your campaign committee and also have them pass out a brochure. If anyone needs to be registered, help him or her.

Another way to organize registration drives is to get lists of people who have been recently added as customers from utility companies. Send workers out to these houses. But the important point is to have a plan before you proceed.

If you are in a state were registration is fairly easy, you or your workers can simply hand out registration forms. Help people fill them out and be sure to take them or mail them to the proper election office. In some states, like Illinois, only deputy registrars may register people. In that case, you would have to go to the county clerk and become deputized. Also, in some states the precinct committeemen automatically can register people. In any event, find out what the law is and be sure you comply. Remember, every vote is important, and at the same time you and your workers are doing an important civic "good deed."

Reward people who register the most people to vote during your campaign committee meetings. For example, give away a free dinner for two to the top registration "getter." Often times, you can find merchants who will give away prizes as a promotion.

Letters to clubs and organizations is another campaign activity that can be started in the middle of the campaign. In a campaign for governor, I was given the job of organizing letters to clubs and organizations in our county. I must admit that I wasn't too excited about the assignment at first, but after we started to get things organized, I got very excited.

I started by making a list of clubs and organizations in the area; for example, medical organizations, business clubs, social clubs and school-related clubs—anything I could think of. Next, I started contacting the president or other leaders of the clubs or group. I also got lots of ideas about who to contact from other members of the campaign committee during the weekly meeting. In fact, getting names was easy. This is just one of the many benefits of the weekly meeting.

When I called, I was direct. After I identified myself and my candidate, I asked:
1. "Would you write a letter of support?"
2. "Would you give us your mailing list?"
3. "Would you let us mail the letters to your members?"

Many of these leaders agreed and wrote letters and gave us the mailing lists. If fact, I was a little surprised how easy it was to coordinate this activity. Next, the committee mailed the letters to the people on this list.

One leader even donated the stamps and mailed the letters himself!

This proved to be an excellent way to spread the word about our candidate and, depending on how involved you want your campaign to be, you may want to consider this too.

Many businesses "market" their products using this networking technique and consider it the best. Americans tend to be club "joiners" and oftentimes can be influenced by appealing to group loyalties. A good example of this at the national level in elective politics is the endorsement of presidential candidates by union leaders.

Your campaign is in full swing now and you are ready to move into the final phase. Your committee should start meeting every week until election day.

In summary, you should have lots of ideas now for your campaign activities. The following activities should be considered in the middle of your campaign:
1. Coffees
2. Advertising
    a. Yard signs
    b. Letters to The Editor
    c. Endorsements
    d. Brochures
    e. Newspaper ads
    f. Radio and TV ads
3. Voter registration drives
4. Letters to groups

NOTES

Chapter 11

Final Campaign Activities
The Countdown

By now, your campaign is in high gear and the finish line is in sight—election day. In this chapter, several final campaign activities will be introduced:

1. Telephoning your supporters and others and reminding them to vote.
2. Networking with friends.
3. Poll watching and follow-up.
4. Showing appreciation to poll-watchers and election judges.
5. Driving people to the polls.
6. A victory celebration.

Abraham Lincoln said there are really only two important campaign activities: first, find out who is supporting you; then second, make sure they vote. This phase of the campaign should concentrate on the second activity of making sure that your supporters vote.

Start by gathering the lists you have been keeping—the lists of people who signed your petition, the list of people you visited door-to-door or met at social or political functions and everyone who has helped your campaign whether by monetary support or as a part of your committee. Then assign someone to consolidate those lists and look up the phone numbers. You want to be ready to start calling around two or three days before the election; so plan accordingly.

Plan a script of what will be said on the phone calls. For example: "Hello, my name is _____ and I am working on _____'s campaign committee. (pause and wait for a response) Election day is Tuesday and _____ (first name of candidate) would appreciate your support. Do you know where the polls are or do you need help getting there?"

Notice that the script is simple. People get irritated if a caller goes into a long dissertation on their cause. Also, the call should be helpful. You are giving information when voting will take place and how to get there. Have a list of polling places and information about voting available for each caller. You'd be surprised how many people don't know where to vote and in some cases how to vote. For example, we moved from Illinois to New York and found the voting procedures very different.

Pick a date to call, usually two or three days before the election. Try to find a central place to call from where all your volunteers can meet. Plan your calls at night from around 7:00–9:00 P.M. to avoid suppertime and bedtime. Each person should be able to call at least 50 people in an hour. So if you have 1,000 people on your list, you will need ten people calling. If it is impossible to schedule this because you don't have enough phone lines, break it into several nights.

You should try to find a location with several phone lines. Real estate offices have worked well for committees I've worked with. Usually the political regulars will know of places and will point them out to you. It is important to keep your volunteers together in one location and working on the same night (if possible). I have observed that if you let people call from their own homes, at their leisure, they either will not make the calls or call when it is convenient for them—which may or may not be convenient for the person receiving the call. Calling is an important activity and should be handled carefully. Offensive calls during dinnertime could end up giving votes to your opponent.

A final note about calling: Bring coffee and snacks for the callers. Create a light social atmosphere. After the calling, plan a party for those who can stay. Be sure to invite these people to your victory celebration—but more on that later.

Also, there are several other ways to organize the phone calling. One is to telephone all registered voters in the election district—if you have the resources to do this. Another is to call all members of certain clubs or organizations.

It also can be worthwhile to ask everyone on your committee to call a number of their friends (say ten) and ask them to vote. This has a networking-type effect and can create a lot of excitement for the candidate.

However, I would not substitute these kind of activities for the calling of people on your lists. The key here is to focus on calling people you know will vote for you. You will get better results calling people you already know are your supporters. A "shot gun" approach could backfire and generate support for your opponent. Remember again what Abraham Lincoln advised—find out who your supporters are and get them to vote.

You may think that at election day your campaign will be over. Not so. There is one final activity that could be crucial to your election. Remember, history has shown countless elections that were won by only a few or even one vote!

Poll watching can be very important to your campaign and in addition it is fun. You need to find at least one person who will act as a poll watcher in each polling place. You will also have to get credentials from the local voting authorities ahead of time, so plan for this.

The poll watcher sits in the polling place next to the election judges and watches for irregularities. For example, it is unlawful to conduct campaign activities or have signs posted for a candidate near or at a polling place. The poll watcher also makes sure that "real" voters vote. Someone with a good knowledge of the local area would be a good candidate. However, most important for your campaign, the poll watcher takes your list of supporters to the polls—broken down by polling area and checks off people as they vote. Near the end of the day with about two hours left to vote, the poll watcher should call a central number where you will have callers ready and "report" which of your supporters haven't voted. Your callers then place a follow-up call and remind the supporters how critical their vote is and ask them to vote.

This activity isn't always practiced in modern day America, but it was a key activity in the past. Big city machines used poll watchers to "milk" every vote possible. I have worked on several campaigns where this was used successfully. Many people will "promise" to vote—even a day before the election—but forget to vote election day. A little nudge can help.

We used poll watching in the first precinct where I was precinct committeeman. As a result, our precinct had one of the highest turnouts (for our party) in the county.

A final note on this: On election day, have someone from your committee stop early in the morning at the polling places and deliver donuts or other treats. The underpaid election judges and your poll watchers will love it—and they will probably be sure that you get a "fair shake" in the election.

Also, it would be a good idea to have several volunteers who are available to drive people to the polls.

Elderly people and the handicapped many times want to vote but can't because of their physical condition. Get the names from your earlier phone calling.

Now comes the hard part. You've spent months, maybe years preparing for and executing your campaign and now it's all coming down to one thing—people will vote and you will win or lose. All you can do is wait until after the polls close and find out the final results. You should be optimistic and have planned a victory celebration well ahead of time so your supporters can wait together—in a party atmosphere to find out the final vote.

The victory celebration can also serve as a "thank you" from you for all the work done by your supporters. Be sure every supporter and member of your committee is invited. Plan for a long evening especially when some votes have to be counted by hand. Set up radios or televisions for people to watch the results. Also be prepared with appropriate statements for the press who also may attend.

A note here: It is OK to expect to win. A positive attitude can work wonders throughout the election. However, if you don't win, lose gracefully. There will be another day. People will respect you more and be more willing to help you in future campaigns if you act like an adult if you lose the election.

Good Luck!!!

In summary, you should have considered the following campaign activities in the final stages of your campaign:
1. Telephoning your supporters and others and reminding them to vote
2. Networking with friends
3. Poll watching and follow-up
4. Showing appreciation to poll-watchers and election judges
5. Driving people to the polls
6. A victory celebration

NOTES

CHAPTER 12

SUMMARY

This book was designed to take you in chronological order through the steps it takes to get elected to political office. The underlying goal is to help you get elected.

In Chapter 1, the considerations of choosing an office were discussed.
- Is it feasible to win?
- What is the political climate?
- Do you really want to do the job?
- What will be the effects on your family?

Chapter 2 suggested shortcuts to office.
- Be appointed to fill an unexpired term.
- Convince the incumbent to retire.

Chapter 3 outlined how to put on your best face.
- Assess your strengths and weaknesses.
- Have good health.
- Have a good appearance.
- Have appropriate clothing.

- Read books on politics.
- Have good campaign material, such as business cards, resume, and a photo.

In Chapter 4, laying the groundwork was discussed.
- Get lists of people to help.
- Establish a calendar of events and attend these events.
- Help in other campaigns.
- Become a party "regular."

In Chapter 5, choosing a campaign manager was discussed.
- It is important to have one.
- Don't choose your spouse.
- Prepare a job write-up.
- Ask local political leaders for advice.
- Pick someone who will add "balance" to the campaign.
- Make a selection.

In Chapter 6, several ideas for getting started were presented.
- Pick a very few people to help at first.
- Schedule a campaign meeting.
- Appoint someone treasurer.
- File petitions.
- Announce your candidacy.
- Hold a press conference.
- Send an announcement letter.

In Chapter 7, several ideas on building the campaign organization were introduced.
- Find people who love politics to help.
- Appoint department heads.
- Have regular meetings.
- Plan an agenda for the meetings.

The strategy of the campaign is discussed in Chapter 8.
- Develop a theme.
- Create a brochure or hand-out.
- Emphasize your strengths.
- Add the unexpected.
- Don't over-sell.
- Consider timing of the campaign.

Chapter 9 outlined early campaign activities.
- Having a fund raiser.
- Attending meetings and events.
- Establishing a newsletter.
- Starting door-to-door campaigning.

Middle campaign activities were introduced in Chapter 10.
- Coffees.
- Advertising.
  - Yard signs.
  - Letters to the Editor.
  - Endorsements.
  - Brochures.
  - Newspaper ads.
  - Radio and TV ads.

- Voter registration drives.
- Letters to groups.

Chapter 11 included the final campaign activities.
— Telephoning your supporters and others and reminding them to vote.
— Networking with friends.
— Poll watching and follow-up.
— Showing appreciation to poll-watchers and election judges.
— Driving people to the polls.
— A victory celebration.

NOTES

EPILOGUE

Keep it Going

Well, it's all over and in all probability you're now starting a new phase in your life—service in public office. But even if you didn't win, it's time to step back and evaluate the situation. You've probably grown a lot as a person, you've learned a lot about the political process and you've probably made more friends than you thought you'd ever make. You need to ask yourself: "Was it worth it? Would you do it again?" If you answer "yes," don't forget that you have created a great campaign team. Don't forget them.

You should have already sent out personal thank you notes to all your supporters and campaign workers. In addition, plan to get the group together periodically in the future. Your campaign should have become some sort of a "social" event and most people would appreciate keeping it going. In fact, if you intend to stay in politics, which I suspect you will, you will need this group again to get elected or to go for a higher office.

Good luck with your new endeavors!!!

APPENDIX 1

1. Ailes, Roger. *You Are the Message*. Homewood, IL: Dow Jones-Irwin, 1988

2. Carnegie, Dale. *The Quick and Easy Way to Effective Speaking*. Garden City, New York: Dale Carnegie & Associates, Inc., 1962

3. Elgin, Suzette Haden. *The Gentle Art of Verbal Self Defense*. Boulder City, NV: Dorset Press, 1980

4. Matthews, Christopher. *Hardball*. New York: Harper & Row, 1988

5. McGinniss, Joe. *The Selling of The President 1968*. New York: Trident Press, 1969

6. Nimmo, Dan D. *Candidates and Their Images: Concepts, Methods and Findings*. Pacific Palisades, CA: Goodyear Publishing Company, 1976

7. O'Connor, Edwin. *The Last Hurrah*. Boston, MA: Little Brown, 1956.

8. Parkinson, Hank. *Winning Political Campaigns and Publicity*. Wichita, KS: Campaign Associates Press, 1973

NOTES

ORDERING INFORMATION

If you would like to order *So You Want to Run for Political Office*, see the ordering information below.

Call or write us for information about quantity discounts or seminars on getting elected.

Also, we welcome your comments and suggestions.

Order Form

Greenfield Center Press
3 Brookstone Drive
Greenfield Center, NY 12833
(518) 893-7974

(Make check payable to
Greenfield Center Press)

Book $12.95

Postage and handling . .$ 1.75

Subtotal . . . . _____

(NY Residents add the applicable sales tax on the subtotal) . . . . _____

Total . . . . _____

Name _____

Address _____

City _____ State _____ Zip _____

Please allow six to eight weeks for delivery. Price subject to change without notice.

NOTES